Resistance

Resistance

reflections on survival, hope and love

Poetry by William Morris
Photography by Jackie Malden

Westphalia Press
An Imprint of the Policy Studies Organization
Washington, DC
2022

Westphalia Press
An imprint of Policy Studies Organization
1527 New Hampshire Ave., NW
Washington, D.C. 20036
info@ipsonet.org

ISBN: 978-1-63723-811-0

Cover and interior design by Jeffrey Barnes
jbarnesbook.design

Daniel Gutierrez-Sandoval, Executive Director
PSO and Westphalia Press

Updated material and comments on this edition
can be found at the Westphalia Press website:
www.westphaliapress.org

For Veronica

Crescit Eundo

Contents

Write

Write.
What shall I write?
That all men are thieves and fools,
And all women foolish?
That tomorrow, like today, mirrors yesterday?
That hope must conquer expectation,
Lest fear have dominion?
That good is embattled,
Whereas evil abounds?
And that peace is ephemeral,
Or that kind words are short and easy to speak,
But that their echoes are endless.

On Survival

Look over the Edge

Beyond the pale lies
Darkness,
Or light?
Day,
Or night?
And do you care?
Or do you dare,
Not be bothered?

Oblivion
Would be God's fault
Should it happen.

Dying is like a sledge,
Falling off a mountain.
It's either fun, or fatal.

Eden

Eden's serpent had a fatal beauty,
As the desert and the raging sea.
We are not bystanders to these awesome creatures,
For each finds a home in me.

Soft, smooth hope rends tomorrow,
Unheard, unspoken dreams shape the world;
Webs of despair catch teardrops of sorrow,
Whilst sunlight in shards, by the broken gets hurled.

On the disappearance of the Merlin[i]— a lament

Swift, knife, heart cut bird,
Why have you gone, where then blood of mine?

The hedge is empty, bare undressed by your absent savagery.
Speed blade runner, giving death and hope,
Spitfire-winged, and hearted, kind killer.
Where then?
Could a curse on your slaughterer release you from fast
extinguished oblivion?
Then let it be so.
Sweet precious lightning streak, you are worth killing for little
killer.
The hills are empty, dead without you.
Without you here they hold but sadness like the memory of a
long-gone, half-remembered dream,
The half-forgotten touch of a lost but cherished lover, dead
and decayed in might-have-beens, and crass futility.

Like a dark cut starburst you were life-giving and sustaining.
In comparison an arrow is tardy, a bullet graceless.
Ground hugging killer, daytime death lover,
Little frail one, harbinger of anarchy and glory,
For the absence of the small death, the great death comes
closer
—and mankind doesn't even notice.

Scimitar winged and dead—the just obliterated.
At whose volition?
Scythe hedge and grass, brashing the trees with your death
flight.
Blood herald wingtip touch the ground again.

Live again,
That the earth may offer up her sacrifice to you.
Your action, disappearance, is without right,
Merciless is the merciless.

Return little killer, turn again swift.
Tear at the guts of your prey at your killing post.

Swift again swift,
Lest the soul of our being shrivel just a little
For the lack of you,
As each further lack shrivels mankind,
And our death rattle, like yours, moves inexorably closer.

Taste

Taste life,
Watch it,
Drink it in when times are good.
Stand and stare,
And live every instant.

But when the sky crashes down,
And oppression weighs heavy on your shoulders,
Run.
Get away.
Escape elsewhere.
Or summon strength,
Turn and fight,
If you must.

Which is fine.
But don't,
Do as I do,
And endure.

Don't Die in the Dark

The world expects you'll yet stand tall,
As all within you crumbles,
You've not the heart to live at all,
Your Spirit's crushed and feeling small,
Your aching body stumbles.

Could you but scream it might begin,
Your hoped for expiation,
But you're completely steeped in sin,
Your broken soul seems dark within,
No hope of reparation.

So pause a moment and step back,
From the abyss that beckons.
Truth is there's nothing that you lack,
So cast the burden from your back,
What e'er the cost it reckons.

Drink from the water of the stream,
And cleanse your mind with daylight.
However dark the storm may seem,
Blink wide your eyes and shed the dream,
And see the past as star bright.

Living

God. Won't you answer?
Won't you tell us why,
Why you hurt children,
And make mothers cry?

Should we not blame you?
Is it not your fault?
We'd name and shame you,
Could it make you halt.

We'd in frustration,
Tear the world apart,
Would that but change things,
Help the healing start.

We love creation.
Are you not the same?
We'd give oblation,
Even take the blame,
Would you but stop this,
Could you only mind,
Heal all the madness,
Stop us feeling blind,
And then help us find,
An answer.

Evil

Infinite world,
Stretches away.
Infinite evil,
Still holds sway.
Infinite mind,
Deep within,
Infinite hope and infinite sin.[ii]

What then does God think?
What could he say?
If there's hope in the future,
Where's the love in today?

In this world without end,
Can good never begin?
Life's blood seeping out,
Whilst the Devil creeps in.

High and Mighty

He built a castle in the sky,
And wove it full of wonder.
The towers were out of emeralds cut,
Bedecked and clothed with splendor.
And there he sat and watched the world,
Far, far below meander.
The people with their cares and woes,
He all assessed with candour.
Their rank ambitions great and small,
Were nothing if not noble.
Their sadness and their hopes and fears,
He loved them all and wept their tears,
And noted each small trouble.

But they were there and he was here.
He never walked amongst them.
He never saw what they would see,
He couldn't be what they could be,
As their lives broke asunder.

And he was great and they were small,
Of that much he was certain.
But to the dust they all would come,
Their journeys would one day be done,
And who would then remember,
That castle and its splendor?

Waiting Longer

God watches,
Satan waits,
And us we muddle on.
Nothing seems to make much sense,
There is no right or wrong.

Could we but change the all of it,
Could we but start again,
We'd only make a hash of it,
As we did way back when.

This now is the beginning,
The start, the end, the new,
The day we mold is tarnished,
The task is for the few.

There is no need for good men,
They've stood by long enough,
This work is for the broken,
For only they are tough.

Amor Vincit Omnia

When storms blow hard, stand fast, stand firm
And never bend or bow,
Lest they rip out the guts of you,
And thus your Spirit cow.

The pain, the pain, the pain of it,
Will crush your soul to dust,
Unless you turn defiantly,
As God demands you must.

The dogs that nip and tuck your heels,
Are bolstered by your fear.
So turn and face and stare them down,
And they will each stand clear.

This world is broken, that we know,
Unleash the hounds of hell,
To put things right should not give pause,
Catharsis makes things well.

The more the storm, the worse the threat,
The stronger you shall grow,
Until the starbright power of love,
Subsumes you in its glow.

Her

Don't cross her, she'll betray you.
She whispers at your heart,
Snake wraps your very being
And rends your soul apart.

Her lips taste like the Ice Queen's
Both small and luscious red.
They promise love and solace,
But offer pain instead.

Her voice is like an angel's
Bright shining as the sun,
Her siren's song's delusion,
Brings death if you don't run.

Her hands you yearn to hold fast,
Quite half as small as mine.
Her tongue is like a serpent's
Part devil, part divine.

Her eyes are laced with heartbreak,
They rend brave men apart.
Prey taunted by this tigress,
Her play right from the start.

Her hair could best Medusa's,
Who broke hearts by the score.
Left them carved in ice cool stone,
Left them broken and alone,
In pain forevermore.

Paradise Lost

And now she's gone, she's gone forever,
Her hand from mine was ripped.
She loved us once—now, then and ever,
But from the world she's slipped.

The many that were lost before her,
The places, times and friends,
Cannot be grasped and measured whether,
You'd yet still try to mend,

To mend the loss and build things better,
And let the dark day end.
No remedy, no magic clever,
Will bring you back dear friend.

The pastures green,
The paths we've seen,
They've gone to not return.
The world spins on,
The past is gone,
And much that's good will burn.

And yet there's yet a new beginning,
Firm ground beyond the mire,
And pastures new you'd not have wandered,
Had you stayed by the fire.

So seize the day and love forever,
You've still a while to live,
And what you have, with joy surrender,
You've far more yet to give.

Dragon Slaying

Her trembling hand caressed the glistening blade,
And thrust it deep into her dragon breast.
That oft regarded fire within her stayed,
Damped not extinguished, hers no mortal rest.
She fed on fear just as she fed on love,
But cut her through with hatred and she'd gasp,
And clutch her heart and tremble like a dove,
Crushed carelessly within an infant's grasp.

Grace undiminished then she leaves the stage,
And Pyrrhic sunlight soft restores my soul.
Her end demarks the opening of a page,
Thus new beginnings soothe and make us whole.
The chains that bound us shattering like glass,
The old constraints are washed away like stains,
A new tomorrow shimmers forth at last,
A consolation worthy of our pains.

A cruel freedom this and harshly won,
The comfort thus accomplished tinged with shame.
The shackles that she used not forged but spun,
Care and compassion she would make their name.
Yet freedom's rarely garnered without cost,
Oppressive love is love that must be spurned,
Lest disempowered and crushed we cry too soft
And darkness fills the world we've now abjurned.

We cleave to darkness or we cleave to light,
We reap a whirlwind harsh as any knife.
It takes a war to make us spurn the night,
To dash the poisoned chalice from this life.

Hope and despair adorn a single coin,
And one way or the other it must fall.
God sets the game but we the choice purloin,
And thus our restoration shall not stall.

Dry Bones

The bones I carry on my back,
Are of the homeland that I lack.
I have no place,
No place to be.
I am the nowhere that you see.
Profoundly lost,
My heart unbowed,
The truth I carry is the now,
The now of being,
Being free,
I have no solace but to be.

Should you consider where you are,
If mired in exile, near or far,
Then wonder how you'd be if you,
Were also pressed to start anew.
Could you then lift your heart and sing?
And in so doing angels bring,
To fortify and hold your soul,
Lest you once falter and grow cold?

The day before you, has the past,
Connected, held, within its grasp.
The bones you carry would be yours,
They have no other broken source,
Sing loud, walk tall and soldier on,
There's still a world where you belong,
For all is yours and you are all,
Stand proud, take comfort, and walk tall.

Tomorrow beckons,
Not today,
So laugh and live,
Let others pray.
The demons you are cursed withal,
Have little power, remaining small.
You the tiger, they the mouse,
Seize reassurance,
Phantoms douse.
There's nothing can withstand you now.
No more to fear, or Spirit cow.
Walk on and hold your head up high,
Drink deep hosannas,
Leap,
And fly ...

Perception

Could I but dream tomorrow,
And build a new today.
Could I but reave the stardust,
Re-shape the Milky Way,
I'd hasten me to heaven,
And chase the Angels home,
Then wander through the eons,
Forever would I roam,
Just for the joy of living,
I'd dance among the clouds,
I'd plough the deepest oceans,
And sing such songs aloud.
I'd lay me down in meadows.
I'd wrap me up in flowers.
I'd cherish every sparrow,
To while away the hours.
I'd want no more division.
I'd teach you how to love,
And reconciliation,
Would flow from heaven above.
But I would be so wounded,
If you went your own way;
And war and pain and hatred,
Were always to hold sway.
I'd even walk amongst you,
I'd tell you what to do.
Were it to make a difference,
I'd split myself in two.
I'd die for you beloved,
My precious little child.

My wish is but to help you.
Need you be quite so wild?

Watching tears fall

Teardrops from heaven,
Grace the shape of the world,
The vulnerable broken,
As war gets unfurled.

The high and the mighty,
By hubris defined,
With scant recognition,
That they are unkind.

We'd offer to crush them,
Return hurt for blow,
But that just leaves damage,
You reap what you sow.

Defy and deny them,
Return peace for war,
And do it with courage,
To settle the score.

It may cost you dear though,
A price paid in blood,
And tears of attrition,
Pride dashed in the mud.

But the world that you share,
Will be better by far,
Than the one that God carved,
From the heart of a star.

And the tools we've been given,
Are love, truth and light,
Much stronger than bullets,
They break through the night.

Lord

You stretched the mighty heavens;
You spun the firmament;

From the sparrow to the behemoth,
all   things
were made
for us.

And yet ...

We are crushed,
Broken,
Bemused,
Bruised by existence,
Troubled, and confused.

Though hope brightens us.

Washed in liquid starlight,
We dream
of a better
Tomorrow

On Hope

Hope

I miss you tree,
Gnarled and beautiful,
Whipping the sky,
You'll outlive me, bold and brazenly, reaching on high,

Though I watch you not, you still grow,
Cleaving heavenward, sweeping low,

Winter naked,
Summer green,
Dressed and undressed, I have seen,
The heart of you,
And I love you,
So.

What's in a Name?

I am what I am.

The boy in the woods with an ocean of tomorrows.

The old one in the forest with a river of yesterdays.

I am sunshine in the Summer that cracks your skin and fills
  your mouth with laughter like the reddest wine.

I am the wind in the darkest Winter's night that reaves your
  soul as the soft rain specks at your face and cleanses
  eternity.

I am lost and I am found.

I am yours and you are mine.

I am Tamburlaine.[iii]

I am Sisyphus.[iv]

I am maybe, perhaps and sorrow.

I am gone before tomorrow.

I am free.

Woman

If I should die,
Or she,
Say this of her,
Or me,
She made me,
Blood of her blood I was born.
And all I do, or have done now,
In her began,
'fore shaped in love by her.

And all I do, or will do,
That too, Is hers, To own,
For good,
Or ill.
For from that birthing comes the will,
That molds us, gives us every skill,
And through her life, inspires ours still.
And makes you what you really are,
A beggar perhaps, or perhaps a star.

Or perhaps the both;
And more,
She shares,
The care,
For all you hold in store,
And shares,
The credit,
For deeds you're yet to do,

Or edit.

The hand that rocked the cradle then,
The hand that started you back when,
And she of her blood, each in turn,
'Til God first set the sun to burn,
And back in time 'til all began,
When, set in motion, we first ran,
She helped us grow and laugh and get,
A new tomorrow and the right,
To face the dawn and fight this fight.

The song we weave,
The life we bring,
Is that selfsame our mothers sing.
She made us then, and paid the cost,
She made the world, the world we lost.
So pause a moment if you can,
And look at her and understand,
Each one of us,
And each to come,
Should oft' remember what she's done,
And say, 'tis woman and was only she,
That made us thus, what we'll yet be.

Remember Her

Come Summer,
Wrap her up,
In goodness.
Soft balm'ed breeze,
Careen her home,
Whilst still alone,
She trails dependents,
Like a fisher girl,
Trails a net,
Behind her.
In evidence of which she holds,
Tomorrow in her hand,
As others did in their time,
She does now,
And stands upon their shoulders in so doing.
So too for all who dare,
To stand defiant 'gainst decree-ed fate,
And cut a path that's ours however late,
A swathe scythed naked from the Summer grass,
For Autumn's coming and comes in too fast.

Yearning

Dance with me Sister Death,
You comfort me,
Like sunshine on the darkside,
You promise a brand new morn.

I'm weary sometimes, just sometimes,
I'm weary of all the pain,
I see in the eyes of others,
Too broken to even complain.

I yearn for a brand new tomorrow,
For Elysian Fields and for love,
But there's still an ocean of sorrow,
Between me and my god far above.

Yet there's beauty in the painfulness,
There are roses in the dung,
So I'll wait a little longer,
Before this dance is done.

Our condition

Like a knife you cut us,
Shrieve^v us 'till we're bare,
Like a newborn, naked,
Not that you would care.

Careless of our stature,
You cut us down to size,
The God we love and worship,
Is ruthless, damn His eyes.

Would you have us broken,
Then build us up again?
Your word is never token,
You crucify mere men.

Yet still we want and need you,
Still we hold you fast.
We have no other option,
Be this our final gasp.

And so, we will obey you,
Though riven through with sin;
This contest so uneven,
That we can never win.

Defiance

The sun beats cold into a heart,
Left naked like the wintered trees,
Stripped bare and hungry for the Spring,
Denied the warmth that day might bring,
And wounded by the dart,
That none but Perseus[vi] sees.

Yet could Medusa's ice queen grip,
Be loosened by mere tears of blood,
Could Dido[vii] thrust forth lilied ground,
For each new day without a sound,
Lest through each heart would rip,
The Sunbane[viii] in full flood.

Andromeda[ix] the scant reward,
Mere vessel for a Summer's spawn,
Now pregnant with a verdant green,
Replete, soft spoken and obscene,
Too much to yet afford,
The Hermes[x] herald dawn.

Could I not stem the tide of death,
That all this lusciousness foretells,
I'd roar Canute-like at the sea,
And bend great Neptune's ancient knee,
And with my dying breath,
Reive Hades[xi] of his spells.

For you there's nothing I'd not do,
I'd pinion Christ; the world would stop,
I'd crush the gods beneath my heel,

And make the wretched Furies[xii] squeal,
Could I but salvage you,
I'd damn the unseen crop.

But that's a dawn we'll never see,
The gods drink deep and drink their fill,
They'll take us down but we can fight,
For truth 'gainst evil and the right,
To let our children be,
Not bend them to their will.

Trembling

Touch a leaf and it trembles,
Touch a life and it bends,
Touch today, it dissembles,
Touch tomorrow, it mends.

What I give, you just borrow,
Unrequited am I,
Where you lead, I but follow,
Snatching hope, lest I die.

In the darkness, you find me,
In the still, quiet word,
With your questions, you bind me,
Now just let me be heard.

Existential

What is love,

if we no longer breathe,

the freshening air of Springtime, that shakes the gossamer but
   so soon ragged wing of the butterfly?

What then is love in the dark embrace of clay, decay, and fast
   forgotten yesterday?

Love is the fire on the altar of your heart, that none shall ever
   extinguish.

Never,

because they cannot,

because you have been,

and therefore you are.

And even though you be a sparrow, storm tossed above the
   ocean of eternity, with no place to rest,

Doomed to an uncomfortable end,

Still you exist,

because you have once existed,

and no one, not even God, shall ever, ever, take that away
   from you.

The Eternal Quest

Could we but cut these surly bonds whilst heavenward
    leaping,
Could we but gaze beyond the sweep of mortal man,
Could I but die and dying know a new tomorrow,
Could you but strive to understand me if you can.

Then we would know and knowing be the freshening ocean,
Then we could swim and understand the deep so clear,
Then we could navigate and sail the very heavens,
Then we could hear the music of the farthest sphere.

And should peace come, as well it could with such a solace,
And should we be far better still than we have been,
And should the striving that consumes be then abolished,
And should there be no need to truck with mortal mien,

I do not doubt that therein lies the smallest maybe,
The hope of peace, and peace could bring an end to fear,
But truth to tell, there'd still be ground for mortal weeping,
I'd not relinquish those that once had held me dear.

And there's the rub we sometimes call misunderstanding,
And knowing you, and moreso yet, still knowing me,
Were we to live for e're within the bounds of Eden,
From confrontation, we would still never be free.

For such is such, for all a human precondition,
We best each other when we strive to reach the stars.
It's not for nothing that we are such great achievers,
We chase our dreams when oft we are careening far.

And when peace comes, as come it one day must unbidden,
Should we cease breathing as we breathe that breath too deep,
We'd have yet more frontiers to watch and cherish,
And could we still, we'd new worlds now forever reap.

Time

Time
Evaporates,
Trickling away,
Like water,
Running through the fingers of your cupped hands,
Save that with water
You may hold a little back.

Abra Ibrahim

When things are good in Cairo,
When the shisha's burning bright,
When your shoes are getting polished,
And there's whisky in the night,

With the street forever singing,
And your buddy at your side,
Less need for female comfort,
Whilst you watch the ebbing tide,

Of human conversation,
Of hopes and dreams and fears,
Of worldly consternation,
And a universe of tears.

Outside Locanda Windsor,
Across the Square of Dreams,
The world is still your oyster,
And nothing's as it seems.

Could I but rope the heavens,
And bring them down to earth,
Take all the wealth of nations,
Count that of little worth.

There'd be no greater comfort,
Than to rest here at the last,
Watch sand slip through your fingers,
And contemplate the past.

Take a Chance

There are chances you lose,
And chances you take,
And a far better future,
Is the one that you make.

But however, which and,
Whatever you do,
You still choose and endeavor,
To attempt life anew.

There's hope and there's heart,
And a better road still,
If you have the endurance,
If you just have the will.

But if once you give up,
If surrender you should,
You eliminate maybe,
And all that you could,

And instead crush the Spirit,
And slide towards death,
Which is not our God's purpose,
For the little you've left.

We should live now forever,
And build a new dawn,
And if God then removes us,
We'd still have been born.

Yours the wake of a pebble,
And the world lumbers on,

Your part in it transient,
You at least sang your song.

You lived and you breathed,
And the web and the weft,
Will be brighter by far,
'Cause of all that you've left.

So lift up your heart,
Hook your soul to a star,
The journey's not over,
There's still better by far.

The tomorrows you build,
Are the sum of today,
Fill your heart full with courage,
For you still have your say.

Fight on to the last,
'Till they take you from here,
With determination,
Seize the day without fear.

The sunset that's coming,
Still herald's a dawn,
Look forward not backward,
You've yet to be born.

Like it or Not

Destroy me.
I dare you. Do it.
Do it now then.
Break me in Hellfire,
Burn me,
Bruise me,
Begin me again,
And still —

I remain.
I can be perfect,
But that I doubt
I'll ever give you.
Because
I am,
Yours as I am,
To use.

Which you do,
Destroy me I mean.
Or do you not?
Inch by little inch,
We fall,
Brute Dashed,
Against the rocks,
Of time.

I care not.
Though darkness call,
And there be no
Awakening,

I remain with you,
My Destroyer,
My Maker,
And My God.

Wait

Wait.
And waiting, watch,
And thinking, think,
Slow turns the world,
And never stops,
Nor should it,
Could it wish to.

Throw a pebble in the stream,
And watch the ripples spread.
Be thankful that you're still alive,
You'll be a long time dead.

Don't Blink

Time passes,
Each drop fresh squeezed from the heart of eternity,
Like a pip from an orange,
Like the blood of Christ.
And life takes over,
In lotus eating,
Fast beating,
Redolent somnambulance.

Could I but carve a space out,
A place out,
Of time,
And in that refuge do the things I should have done,
Would have done.

The things that weren't,
Because there was no time.
Adventures lost,
Words unwritten,
Spitten bitter out,
With time's fast passing.

Passing

The world about me grows young,
As I grow older,
It seems I've scarcely begun,
Yet I grow colder.
Invisible hands transform city streets,
And where it was higgledy, now it is neat.
And people grow younger,
Stronger,
As I grow old,
And cold.
Will you love me when I'm done?
With your whole life yet to run?
I'm a memory,
A whisper,
A thought,
Caressed by the wind,
Enfolded by night.
Try not to lose me,
For I am the last,
Of my kind,
Just like you.

Life

As the doe watches the tiger,
As the sky watches the earth,
So today yields to tomorrow,
As a child yields to its birth.

There's no end to the beginning.
There's no well in which you fall,
There's no race you need be winning,
Life's the sum total of all.

Listen

Listen then, and listening take heart,
There is no reason to be afraid,
Ever.
For I am with you,
And when you walk, I walk before you,
Cutting a swathe through the world,
Making it easier,
Lest you fail,
To survive.

Secret

Let me tell you what I think,
Not what I think you know,
Of how we hover on the brink,
Not knowing where to go,
That metaphysic link.

When you are eighty-seven,
Perhaps you shall reach beneath the waves
And pick a pebble from the sand,
Which glistens brilliant bright,
In green and blue and maybe white.
And that will be the world, not heaven.

Or when you're ninety-six,
A faery child,
With eyes forlorn, and wide, and mild,
Will smile at you,
And lead you to a wilderness,
And show you how to touch forever.

Or when you're older still,
And busy writing, thinking hard,
Then thought will take you by the hand,
And take you to a place transcending time,
in which,
a door, or perhaps a box,
contains the universe,
wrapped in a ball,
that sparkles.

The secret truth not many know,
Is that the world has angels,

Big as houses,
Bigger still,
And coloured black, or gold, and sometimes white,
With giant wings and friendly faces,
Watching you,
Kindly,
All the time.

Now

I ache to find a new tomorrow,
Break with all that's been,
And abnegate the sands of sorrow,
To fight the more I'm keen.

Could I but reach and catch an angel,
Catch one by the hand,
And laugh and put her in my pocket,
And never let her land?

Could I stretch up and touch a rainbow,
Pluck it from the sky,
Could I but hold a wodge of stardust,
The Pleiades I'd try.

But I've got pockets full of angels,
Stardust in my eyes,
And now I've caught another rainbow,
That sure is a surprise.

On Love

Purpose

It is love that drives us forward, through the darkness,
   through the night,
Yet it's greed's remorseless shadow that still shades us from
   the light.

Is it power that all will covet, as we forge ahead to death?
And what solace will it give us, as we gasp our final breath?

Is it hope of life hereafter that sustains us in the cold?
Will it give us all true courage, as we weaken and grow old?

Only love is the redeemer. Only love casts out all fear.
Selfless love sustains the angels — and all those that
   we hold dear.

Holding on

Love is the whisper on the wind that brings balm and solace
to ease remembered pain.

Love is the sunshine in the morning that banishes the night
and brings the fresh'ning rain.

Love is hope, and love is sorrow, love is song still here
tomorrow. Love is everything and more, and love is true.

What is the point of being sad, being happy, being glad, and
of anything at all, if there's not love?

It's love that makes the planets spin, makes your heart beat
deep within, and then heals the tears of Sin, merely love.

For without it nothing works, not this world with all its
quirks, nor would God such comfort be, were not there
love.

Love sustains the all that is, and the joy that laughter gives,
love is everything that is, only love.

Could I?

Could I but be the apple of your eye,
Then rainbows I would carry,
And cast them at your feet,
I'd build you bowers of stardust,
And make your days replete,
Could you but love me.

Could I but break the chains that hold you fast,
Then daydreams I would gather,
And weave them in your hair,
I'd wrap you round with moonbeams,
Your troubles I would bear,
Could you my love be.

Could I but bend your mouth into a smile,
I'd build you songs of sunlight,
And shape them to your lips,
Like kisses mixed from music,
To share with you in sips,
Lest you my love see.

Could I but hold you close and keep you near,
I'd pave your way with flowers,
And bathe you in their dew,
Like mountains squeezed from teardrops,
Shed for the love of you,
Lest you not want me.

Fading Love

Deep within she may perhaps think,
Of the warmth that someday might link,
Her heart to mine lest we grow cold.
So loving her, I long to hold,
Her close, that she may yet obey,
The instinct that must in her grow,
To feel secure, that she may know,
How gentle is this life of ours.

How senseless it seems now to cower,
At the loneliness of the night,
For in her solemn eyes a light,
May yet fill up that emptiness,
That strives to make me something less,
Than could be were her cautious heart,
To garner rather than to start,
And hold but then draw back again,
Before the love that seeks in vain,
To keep her safe from the real world.

The Love I Voice

You bow your head; I ache for the lack of you.
Your eyes glance down and wrench my breath away.
Then stirs a passion, tender, frail and new,
Fresh as the sunrise at the break of day.
Just so you touch and tear apart my heart,
As you have done these many times and more.
In half a heartbeat then I'd up and start,
Fey like some buck deer frightened to the core.
I would stand shameless but that I might fail,
And thus I'm doomed to quell my nascent love.
For you such daunting play will never pale,
For thus the hawk is tressed down by the dove.
Unleashed, this fever I'd no more restrain,
Thus for protection, you'll indifference feign.

The love I voice, bare hides an aching need,
To somehow take and hold you for my own.
Your conjured image leads my heart to bleed,
At uncommitted sins I should atone.
I'd catch the stars and throw them at your feet,
Tress you with rainbows, could I count you mine.
Clothe you with sunlight, manna you would eat,
You'd bathe your limbs in lakes of moonlight fine.
Sweet expiation I'd find in your eyes,
With flowers and larksong I would fill your days.
I'd swim the ocean if you were the prize,
Climb any mountain just to earn your praise.
I'd find redemption, could you make me whole,
Could I contrive to win your heart and soul.

I love you like the wind adores the rain,
I love you more than sunshine, more than hope.
Were you to spurn me, I'd love you again,
If loved by you, with hellfire I could cope.
I'll cherish every inch there is of you,
I'll worship and adore you from afar.
My love is resurrected ever new,
There's naught you'd do my love could ever mar.
With consolation you'd my heart beguile,
To stand beside you, battle I would dare,
To spare you I would suffer any trial,
The very spoils of life with you I'd share.
I love you as the ocean loves the shore.
It's you I love for now and evermore.

Loving

Touch my heart,
And I yearn,
As does any man.

Steal my heart,
And I cry,
As would you.

Wound my heart,
And I bleed,
As all lovers can.

Break my heart,
And I die,
You would too.

Solace

What then is she?

A woman who could reach and touch the stars and grasp the
Pleiades in the palm of her outstretched hand.

Her courage such that she can fight dragons.

And her compassion great as an ocean for she is built of love,
a testimony to loyalty and indomitable joy.

This special, this rare creature, the weft and warp of whom
is love,

Is pure magic, like a sparkle with a dash of stardust,

And a splash of sunshine,

And a shimmer of laughter,

And all the hope,

And joy,

That ever was,

In all God's universe.

The Days Run Fresh with Love

The hope in you,
The smile in you,
The shine, the new beguile in you,
These, make me love you.

The freshening day,
The things you say,
That joy your laughter brings my way,
With you forever will I stay,
Lest from my side, you ever stray.
So I, must love you.

Like the moon loves the sun,
Like the ocean loves the shore,
Like tomorrow loves before,
Thus, you still, I adore.

Perfect Love

When is love not selfish,
Serving want not need?
When is love not cruel,
Ruthless in its creed.

When is love not painful,
Hurtful when denied?
Fostering resentment,
Reiving through our pride.

Though real true love's an ocean,
In which we all should drown,
The succor and redemption,
We seek this life to crown.

We'd pluck it from the rafters,
Or dredge it from the sea,
We'd fight with God to find it,
It's all that makes us free,

To truly love each other,
The flame that bests the dark,
The loved one and the lover,
The arrow and the mark.

The Sun

Like the sun you smile at me,
Like the stars you laugh.
Hope is in the memory,
All that is our history,
The tender world you craft.

Could we build a universe,
Weave it out of love,
Then my heart would gentler be,
Freed to sing in harmony,
Soaring like a dove.

Tomorrow

In the soft curve of the desert sand,
I watch your lithe and supple body.
As I walk this humid sun-drenched land,
I feel the warmth of you about me.
While I sink beneath the crystal brine,
I listen for your sparkling laughter.
When I touch the darkness sharp and fine,
I sense the strength of love hereafter.
If I take hold of the crescent moon,
I know you're in the brightening whiteness.
Could I catch a fiery, star-dark tune,
I'd see you in the flashing lightness.
How the desert sunset draws me on,
With love's raw, red, chaste heat so fearsome.
Hear the sand-sharp winds sing softening song,
To match my lonely, broken heartbeat.

Remembered Love

Sweltering, summer heat,
Slippery with redolent sweat,
Summons remembrance of you.

Your eyes, doe like, entrancing,
Your hair, as it once was, long, cascading,
Your body lithe,
Your laughter, like a river,
Your smile, like sunshine.

Every gesture, each expression,
A challenge in raw provocation.

Serendipity

Your world turns on a sixpence,
I cannot tell you why,
One moment you are smiling,
The next you start to cry.

Could I but change tomorrow,
I'd change the toughest bits,
Weave joy spun out of sorrow,
And tell you when that it's,
Not to do with me.

Those better, brighter rainbows,
Those deeper, bluer skies,
Those cooler, greener forests,
That gladden your dark eyes.

I'd bring you warmer oceans,
And softer, sandier shores,
I'd glisten them with daydreams,
And then I'd name the cause,
Serendipity.

Light

Light,
Like love,
Cuts deep into
The heart.

Truth,
Like hope's
a foretaste of
Lost joy.

Love,
Like hate's,
held close inside
Your soul.

Love
Is all
God leaves us in
The end.

The Endnotes ...

i   A small species of falcon, known as the pigeon hawk in North America

ii   Jackie's picture is taken in Oxford, England, her home town.

iii   In Christopher Marlowe's play of the same name, Tamburlaine's aspiration to immense power raises profound religious questions as he arrogates for himself a role as the "Scourge of God".

iv   Sisyphus was punished for his self-aggrandizing deceitfulness by being forced to roll a boulder up a hill only for it to roll down when it nears the top, repeating this action for eternity.

v   Shrieve: to free from guilt

vi   Perseus was the killer of Medusa, the Gorgon who turned men to stone.

vii   Dido was the founder and first Queen of Carthage (modern Tunisia). She falls in love with Aeneas and when he leaves her, kills herself.

viii   The Sunbane was a ruinous force in the Chronicles of Thomas Covenant. Kept active by blood sacrifices, the Sunbane had four phases: Fertility, Pestilence, Drought and Rain.

ix   Andromeda was sacrificed by a sea monster but saved by Perseus, who marries her.

x   Hermes is the God of transitions and boundaries. The messenger of the Gods. Took people to the Underworld.

xi   Reive is a word of Scots origin meaning to plunder in a raid. Hades is God of the Underworld.

xii   The Furies (Greek Erinyes) were three netherworld goddesses who avenged crimes against the natural order. They were particularly concerned with homicide, unfilial conduct, crimes against the gods, and perjury.

William Morris

William Morris heads the Next Century Foundation, an international charity devoted to fostering peace and reconciliation in war zones. He is a former broadcaster, editor and publisher. He lives and works in Ludgvan, Cornwall. He is eclectic in his writing, composing everything from nonsense verse to novels, one of which, titled *Springfield the Novel*, was also published by Westphalia Press. Awarded an honorary doctorate by Bolton University for his work promoting peace in the Middle East, William is a frequent traveler to pivotal Mid East countries such as Iraq, Egypt, Gaza, and Libya. William is often accompanied in his travels by Ambassador Mark Hambley, who has acted as an informal ear and critic for this work.

Jackie Malden

Jackie Malden is an artist and photographer based in Oxford, England. She walks every day with her little dog Teddy, and photographs nature ... anything that catches her eye, from the emergence of the smallest wild flower to the vastness and beauty of a sunset. Natural light is the inspiration for many of the images in this book with spring and autumn being favourite seasons. In keeping with her love of nature, she is also a paper collage artist specialising in British birds and wildlife. She exhibits in the annual Oxfordshire Artweeks, and cards of her work sell in shops around the UK as well as online, under her married name Jackie Richards: www.lovefromtheartist.com.

Featured Titles from Westphalia Press

Issues in Maritime Cyber Security Edited by Nicole K. Drumhiller, Fred S. Roberts, Joseph DiRenzo III and Fred S. Roberts

While there is literature about the maritime transportation system, and about cyber security, to date there is very little literature on this converging area. This pioneering book is beneficial to a variety of audiences looking at risk analysis, national security, cyber threats, or maritime policy.

Bunker Diplomacy: An Arab-American in the US Foreign Service by Nabeel Khoury

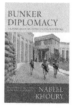

After twenty-five years in the Foreign Service, Dr. Nabeel A. Khoury retired from the U.S. Department of State in 2013 with the rank of Minister Counselor. He taught Middle East and US strategy courses at the National Defense University and Northwestern University.

The Great Indian Religions by G. T. Bettany

G. T. (George Thomas) Bettany (1850-1891) was born and educated in England, attending Gonville and Caius College in Cambridge University, studying medicine and the natural sciences. This book is his account of Brahmanism, Hinduism, Buddhism, and Zoroastrianism

Unworkable Conservatism: Small Government, Freemarkets, and Impracticality by Max J. Skidmore

Unworkable Conservatism looks at what passes these days for "conservative" principles—small government, low taxes, minimal regulation—and demonstrates that they are not feasible under modern conditions.

A Place in the Lodge: Dr. Rob Morris, Freemasonry and the Order of the Eastern Star by Nancy Stearns Theiss PhD

Ridiculed as "petticoat masonry," critics of the Order of the Eastern Star did not deter Rob Morris' goal to establish a Masonic organization that included women as members. As Rob Morris (1818-1888) came "into the light," he donned his Masonic apron and carried the ideals of Freemasonry through a despairing time of American history.

Demand the Impossible: Essays in History as Activism
Edited by Nathan Wuertenberg and William Horne

Demand the Impossible asks scholars what they can do to help solve present-day crises. The twelve essays in this volume draw inspiration from present-day activists. They examine the role of history in shaping ongoing debates over monuments, racism, clean energy, health care, poverty, and the Democratic Party.

International or Local Ownership?: Security Sector Development in Post-Independent Kosovo
by Dr. Florian Qehaja

International or Local Ownership? contributes to the debate on the concept of local ownership in post-conflict settings, and discussions on international relations, peacebuilding, security and development studies.

Geopolitics of Outer Space: Global Security and Development
by Ilayda Aydin

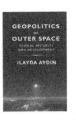

Can an obsession with security pose an ironically existential threat to humanity in this most fragile yet unforgiving environment it is stepping into? This book analyses the Chinese-American space discourse from the lenses of international relations theory, history and political psychology to explore these questions.

Conflicts in Health Policy Edited by Bonnie Stabile,
Introduced by Randy S. Clemons & Mark K. McBeth

When conflicts arise in health policy, policy scholars can contribute to crafting solutions to seemingly intractable problems. Health and medical policy issues require political acumen and policy knowledge to diagnose problems, inform debate, and devise policy interventions.

Poverty in America: Urban and Rural Inequality and
Deprivation in the 21st Century
Edited by Max J. Skidmore

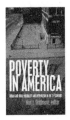

Poverty in America too often goes unnoticed, and disregarded. This perhaps results from America's general level of prosperity along with a fairly widespread notion that conditions inevitably are better in the USA than elsewhere. Political rhetoric frequently enforces such an erroneous notion.

westphaliapress.org

Printed in Great Britain
by Amazon

33641739R00086